BIRTHRIGHT
5 SECRETS TO RECLAIM
THE POWER OF YOU

MARGA MACIAS

I dedicate this book to my children, Paolo and Mika, my pride and joy. Your presence in my life fueled and inspired me to conquer my birthright. I love you with all my heart.

Table of Contents

INTRODUCTION

YOU ARE BORN TO GREATNESS.

T ake a moment to read it again and, even just for a moment, allow that thought to dwell in your mind. YOU ARE BORN TO GREATNESS.

Now, answer me this and be honest with yourself:

How much do you believe that on a scale of one to ten? How convinced are you of that number? Does it fluctuate depending on the day you're having, or are you solid on whatever belief you have?

The reason I ask is that this statement is a 100% truth.

It is a fact as real as you reading this book right now.

Now you may be thinking, *If that is so true, why am I struggling so much? Why aren't things going the way I want them to? Why am I so unhappy? Why am I not successful?*

On a larger scale, you might likewise wonder, *Why is our world the way it is right now? Why is there so much poverty, illness, war, unhappiness, violence, and hatred?*

The answer lies in an enemy among us. It lurks everywhere, sometimes even among the people we love. Some people are not even aware that it is already living within them, growing in strength, until it consumes them like cancer does to one's body.

That enemy spells the difference between merely existing and thriving; between illness and achieving maximum health; between poverty and attaining financial freedom; between mediocrity and limitless accomplishments; between hatred and love; between pain and joy.

That enemy has existed for centuries, creating so much havoc in this world. The problem is, as powerful as it is, no physical weapon can destroy it.

It is menacing in its invisibility. It is a poison that kills one's body and soul.

That enemy has a name. The name is APATHY.

Apathy exists in so many different ways, sometimes without our even knowing it. At some point in our lives, it affected us. For some, it is all consuming and continues to overpower any hope one might have had.

Have you ever been labeled as a procrastinator? Do you frequently have to be reminded to get things done? What about finding it difficult to make a decision without second-guessing yourself constantly? Or deciding on an action but struggle following through?

How important would it be to you to be able to set a goal and go for it with laser focus, saving you time, money, and aggravation? How would it feel to be able to accomplish whatever you set your mind on?

Here's another scenario: Do you avoid interacting with people or shy away from social situations? Does it make you uncomfortable to start conversations with people you don't know, or do activities with new friends?

Imagine having the self-confidence to be able to handle any social situation with ease. Can you see yourself standing tall, smiling, looking people in the eye when you speak and engage confidently with individuals or groups from all walks of life?

What about this: Do you avoid establishing deep relationships with anyone? Is it difficult for you to find sympathy or understand how others feel? Have you shut family or friends away because you have come to the point where you feel like you don't care, maybe because you believe they stopped caring themselves? Do you easily get discouraged or distraught when faced with disappointment?

What would it mean to you to be able to have genuine, meaningful relationships with family and friends without worry or fear? How important would it be to you to know how to relate to and understand people, especially the ones you love? How crucial is having a strong mindset to overcome trials and disappointments in your life?

Has life seemed so unfair to you that you feel like you've given up hope and have stopped trying? Does every road seem like a dead end? Do you want a change but lack the energy to keep going or are at a lost on how to even begin that path?

If you can relate to any of these scenarios, you've come to the right starting place to turn things around with this book.

You see, I've been through all the situations I mentioned—some even more than once. I have struggled, understand the pain, know how it is to feel both hopeless and helpless. I have felt alone, misunderstood, unappreciated.

I get how it feels to feel like you're drowning: drowning in pain, sadness, misery, and despair.

That was then.

Here I am, reaching out to you now: braver, stronger, happier and with a whole new outlook on life, no matter what the past has thrown at me.

My steadfast goal is to share my life journey's lessons with you that helped me survive and become the living, thriving being I am today.

I'm going to take you through the triggers that stand in the way of progress, help you understand pain and how you can embrace it without being shattered.

More importantly, I'm going to teach you five specific secrets to reclaim the power that lives inside you. Once reclaimed, nothing can stop you from being the person you want to be and living the life you hope for.

These secrets are my valuable weapons that allow me to conquer past demons and present obstacles that stand in the way of limitless success in life. Apathy doesn't stand a chance against them, and I'm sharing them with you now.

When you are done, there will be no doubt in your mind that you are born to greatness.

It's your birthright.

The power is in your hands. It's rightfully yours to claim.

CHAPTER 1
That poison called apathy: understanding the enemy

Before I go any further, let's get clear on the enemy called apathy.

By definition, apathy means a lack of feeling, emotion, interest or concern. It comes from the Greek word *apatheia,* which means 'without feeling.' Synonyms include words like emotionless, impassiveness, insensibility, indifference, and numbness.

A Public Library of Science (PLOS) article published in January 2017 defined apathy as a multidimensional condition characterized by decreased motivation, initiation of action and goal-directed behavior.

I believe that apathy is so much more than the words that define it. It is more powerful than we think. I see apathy as a poison, a deep-rooted weed, the ultimate kryptonite that is capable of taking down anyone who allows it into their mind.

Apathy is capable of shattering a person's future and destroying lives. It is the root of many evils in this world we live in. It exists in different forms, each one able to rob individuals of the ability to make wise and well-thought-out decisions for their actions or paralyze them altogether.

Let me go through the different kinds with you.

First, there's Behavioral Apathy. It manifests as difficulty in self-initiated and goal-focused behavior.

There are two problems right from the start: 1) initiating an action, and 2) moving forward to achieve the desired goal. There are the procrastinators. They constantly need to be reminded to get things done and are unable to follow through a decision without much effort and delay.

Meet Ralph. He's 40 years old, has a bachelor's degree in psychology, is happily married with 2 children and has the opportunity to solidify a higher position in his job if he completes a master's degree.

All his life, he has been a procrastinator, waiting until the last minute to get things done—sometimes to the point of letting a golden opportunity pass. He constantly has to be reminded of the importance of the task, urged to get moving.

He would for a few months, then fall back and give a litany of surmountable excuses why he didn't have the time to do things.

"I'm too busy right now. I'm taking care of my kids. I'm supervising a renovation project. My wife needs help. I had to get up early, and I'm so tired. There's not enough time to do that."

This led to frustration from everyone involved: his family, his employer, and even himself. So many crucial chances blown that could have given him the financial stability he and his wife long for.

Next, there's Social Apathy. These are individuals who struggle with social relations. They are the introverts.

They shy away from starting conversations with random people, do not enjoy doing things with new acquaintances and avoid choosing or suggesting activities to do even with their friends. They would rather stay home alone than build helpful relationships.

Have you ever met people who prefer to hide in their shell? They are difficult to engage with because conversations are kept to the bare minimum.

You clearly sense their uneasiness when speaking to them: very brief eye contact; uncomfortable shifting of the body; will only answer questions in 2-3 words but not initiate a conversation; turn down invitations for anything social, and if they do go, stand out like a wallflower.

Lastly comes Emotional Apathy. This group has difficulty with feelings of positive or negative emotion—a term labeled as 'emotional blunting.'

For instance, if they hurt someone or hear bad news, it is not likely for them to feel sad or upset. Neither do they care about what loved ones think of them.

Irene and Karlie are clients of mine. Karlie, the daughter, on the brink of becoming diabetic, bitter and angry about life in general. She was bullied, had very low self-esteem, hated blood sugar checks and resented her mom's efforts to bring her back to health.

It all came to a head one day in my office. Tears are streaming down Irene's face; eyes are deep and dark from lack of sleep. She's begging for help because Karlie sabotages every effort she makes toward improving her health.

Karlie's eyes are narrowed, arrogant, staring off, refusing to look at her mother's face drenched with tears. She lashes out at everyone, to the point of physical aggression toward her siblings. She refuses to look at her mother or me when we speak. Karlie just shut down.

"I don't care," she says over and over again.

My heart ached for Irene who was clearly distraught yet continued to be supportive and loving. Her daughter shut her and everyone off; her face, stone-like; eyes staring out into the distance, so steely cold; arms folded stiffly across her chest.

She created a shield to protect herself from any more pain. She built a wall around her, and she was done feeling and caring.

As multifaceted as apathy is, it also is associated with other conditions which add to the complexity of breaking free from it.

Depression is one of them, with overlapping symptoms like lack of initiative and loss of interest. This combination is common in Parkinson's Disease.

Anhedonia is another associated condition. It is defined as the inability to derive pleasure or a loss of pleasure in activities one used to enjoy. Not surprisingly, it, too, overlaps with depression.

Then there's fatigue, described as a lack of energy to perform actions. It is a feeling of exhaustion from the effort exerted and not related to physical energy from muscle exertion. The effort alone drains you. Again, this is seen in Parkinson's Disease as well as multiple sclerosis.

No one is immune from apathy. Even the healthy population of people can be wrapped in its web. In fact, there are four subtypes of apathy described in this group.

The most common is the Generally Motivated subtype, comprising 61% of the population. The desire exists, but the action is limited by fatigue.

I remember this all too well. I'm 35 years old, a single Mom with two young children, in the middle of my grueling 3-year training in pediatric critical care in Chicago.

My job requires very stressful shifts, sometimes 36 hours long with minimal sleep. I struggle with fatigue, as I try my best to spend quality time with my children whenever I'm home.

I walk into my front door, wanting more than anything to just lie in my bed and close my eyes. I'm greeted by 2 little children so thrilled to see their Mom, bouncing up and down doing the happy dance.

"Mama! I missed you! Can we play?" says my 2-year-old girl, her eyes radiating the 100-kilowatt smile on her face.

"Mama, I have homework, and I want to show you what I made in school," chimes her 6½-year-old brother bringing a handful of papers to me.

How can I say no? My children need me too. I had goals and plans, but when physical, mental and emotional exhaustion took over, the most I could do was function one day at a time. I didn't have the energy to do much more.

The next subtype is the Behaviorally/Socially Apathetic group, affecting 25% of the population. This category is significantly more depressed and fatigued than the other subtypes.

My 58-year-old client Joe has been battling depression for most of his adult life. His parents were quite hard on him, and growing up, he always felt like he wasn't good enough.

"I was expected to follow without question. I felt forced; made to feel like I had to do what they wanted. I tried my best but did not feel appreciated."

He had a failed marriage to a woman who ridiculed him every chance she got and made him feel 'like a loser.'

Eventually, he stopped trying, withdrew into his own world. He no longer socialized, isolated himself even from his family, lost his drive in his business, second-guessed his decisions and was afraid to try anything new.

Then comes the Emotionally Apathetic subtype where 12% of the population fall under. Anhedonia, the inability to derive pleasure or a loss of pleasure in previously enjoyed activities, is more common in this group.

Forty-nine-year-old Monica feels like a victim. All her life she has had a strained relationship with her mother, only a handful of friends she hardly sees and is unhappy with life in general.

She is so overcome with bitterness and resentment that one by one, family and friends start keeping their distance. The more they do, the more she becomes more emotionally detached and loses her desire to connect with and show love to those she once cared about.

Her voice sounds tired, dull, almost lifeless. Her words are pessimistic.

"It's never going to happen. Things are never going to change. This sucks. I'm done. I don't give a crap!"

Her body speaks the same language: slouched against the sofa, stoic face with no light in her eyes, arms folded across like an impenetrable fortress. She truly was done.

Finally, in 2% of the healthy population and thankfully the least common subtype, there is the Generally Apathetic group. These are those who have lost all hope and desire. They have become numb and detached. Nothing matters to them anymore.

They simply exist.

CHAPTER 2
Facing your apathy and taking the reins of control

Whenever a decision is made toward solving a problem or self-improvement, a systematic approach is most helpful.

It begins with a conscious and honest awareness of the problem, identifying and understanding what triggered them in the past, and an unwavering resolve to put the past behind in order to move forward with progress.

I'm going to take you through each step in this chapter. In doing so, pay attention to what resonates with you, what makes you say "Yup, that's me!" Be open and honest with yourself. The more you are, the better you will fully understand how this has weighed you down and fuel you to conquer it.

KNOW YOUR SUBTYPE

Let's get clear on this. Which do you relate to more?

Are you Generally Motivated but drained of energy, tired of trying and not succeeding?

Are you Behaviorally/Socially Apathetic? Do you have a hard time making decisions and following through? Would you rather be alone and find no interest in relationships with people? Do you procrastinate and constantly have to be reminded of your tasks to keep on track?

What about Emotionally Apathetic? Have you lost interest in establishing deep relationships with anyone? Is it difficult for you to be sympathetic and understanding of how others feel?

Are you all of the above and Generally Apathetic?

Take the time to dig deep with no fear of judgment. I've been there myself and understand. There is no shame in admitting to one or all subtypes. The point here is, to overcome it, we must first recognize and know exactly what we're dealing with. Know your enemy first.

IDENTIFYING YOUR PAST TRIGGERS

My own experience and helping thousands of people over the years showed me that there are a few common triggers that stand out. These triggers, especially if they happen repetitively or are constant, usually cause the downward spiral into some type of apathy.

Can they be stopped? Absolutely, but it takes work, and I'm going to show you exactly how.

The most crucial part is reversing that downward spiral before you sink in too deep. Think of it as quicksand or a whirlpool. The deeper you sink, the longer and harder the climb to the surface. This is why it is so important to recognize that descent before you feel as if you're drowning.

Discouragement from Past Attempts and Failures

This is a powerful trigger. I think at some point in our lives, we could all relate to this. The bigger the struggle and more painful the failure, the more it makes us gun-shy. Fear creeps in and can become paralyzing.

This is something I first experienced in my teenage years, and thinking about that time still makes me shudder. You see, I graduated with high honors from high school—#3 in my batch. Straight A student.

Then came college at the age of 16. Pre-Med, to be specific. From a sheltered all-girls school, I transitioned into the top university with thousands of students from all walks of life.

For Pre-Med, it was a dog-eat-dog world because the competition was extremely stiff. The abrupt transition and pressure were overwhelming. I felt like a fish out of water.

Then, for the very first time in my life, I failed my first Chemistry exam.

I remember that moment of horror taking the exam. My mind went blank. Completely blank. Chemistry never worried me in high school but suddenly, in that moment, my mind shut down.

I'm staring at the blue exam booklet that has the University emblem, trembling and on the brink of tears. I can see the question but have no clue where to begin. It might as well be an exam in Greek. My pen is poised on the ruled page, motionless.

I desperately try to pull it together but, instead, feel more panic with each passing minute. I feel my heartbeat pounding even up in my throat. My breathing is fast and shallow. Precious time is lost, and I give up.

I write across the top of the page in all caps, "Mental block. I'm so sorry."

I froze and failed miserably.

That ONE moment and the result crushed me. I lost confidence in myself; self-doubt crept in and was something I struggled with during my 4 years.

I was so stunned and embarrassed. I felt inferior. I went from feeling smart and capable to insecure and scared.

Every exam thereafter became a threat I dreaded, and I failed a few more. That feeling of inferiority greatly stunted my courage to try.

I earned my bachelor's degree in Biology a fraction of a point shy of graduating cum laude. In my young mind, that was a failure.

Looking back now, it was a triumph in itself after 4 years of struggling with my insecurity. It's amazing how powerfully the mind affects everything you do.

Feelings of Unworthiness

This is a tough one. A deep-rooted pain. We all want to be appreciated and loved, and anyone who tells me otherwise is not speaking the truth.

A feeling of unworthiness is a belief that begins when you are made to feel not good enough; when you are constantly criticized, blamed, scolded, humiliated; even mentally, emotionally, or physically abused. In time, the false belief that you are not deserving of love, appreciation, and acceptance creep in, which becomes devastating. When that happens, you resign yourself to pain and misery.

I met my 32-year-old client Gretchen at the height of an emotional breakdown.

I'll never forget how she looked. Pale, so thin from hardly eating; dark circles and sunken eyes from lack of sleep; shaking as if she were standing outside in the dead of winter on that warm, humid summer day.

She looks at me as if someone was pointing a gun at her head that very moment. Sheer terror. She's in an abusive relationship.

Her boyfriend wants to control everything, down to how many almonds she's allowed to eat per day. If she doesn't do as told, he berates and insults her, no matter where they are. At one point, he even grabbed her by the collar and shoved her hard against a wall of a public laundromat for trying to speak her mind.

The longer she stayed with him, the more he broke her spirit until she was a crumpled heap of tears.

Why did she stay? Why did she allow this? She grew up feeling unworthy of her mother's love and that she did not deserve any better.

You see, we unknowingly invite what we manifest. If we manifest unworthiness or low self-worth, we attract someone into our life that brings just what we believe.

The Pain of Rejection

This is another deep-seated pain that can even return to haunt you. It can even paralyze you into moving further with any relationship—for fear of being rejected again.

It's September of 2009. I had just moved cross country to begin a new job. I'm bubbling with excitement because I'm seeing my boyfriend again after 2 months. Surviving my aneurysm a year and a half ago was a wakeup call for us; we reconnect, rekindle the happiness and talk about spending the rest of our lives together.

Our relationship has everything I dream of: respect, love, passion, and emotional support. His green eyes sparkle whenever they look at me.

In the warmth of his arms, I feel comfort, security, and desire. I am so content when he holds me, my head resting on the crook of his neck as we talk about our plans, laughter mixing with kisses on my head or lips whenever I look up at him.

I had no idea that would be the last time I'd see him again.

He was undergoing a personal turmoil I did not know of. When we first met, I was a doctor in training, trying my best to make ends meet and a newly single Mom. He was well established in his job of 30 years and was earning a decent living. He is of Italian descent and old-fashioned standard—where the man worked and the woman stayed at home.

Over the years, the more successful I became, the 'less of a man' he felt, and that was the beginning of the end. He viewed my success as a threat to his masculinity and decided, after 8 years together, that he did not love me enough to move and start a new chapter with me. His reason was, he 'felt castrated' the more self-sufficient I became.

Living in different states, we always made it a point to see each other as often as our jobs allowed. October and November came and went. My biggest shock was when he told me he wasn't going to come in December too, our favorite month together.

He said he was going through a turmoil crisis and needed time away to decide what he wanted to do. No third party involved whatsoever. He asked for space and time without me to cloud his judgment, meaning no phone calls, emails, or text messages either.

Abrupt dead silence, as if he had died.

Picture this. I feel like I'm hit by a bullet train; in total shock and disbelief.

"How the heck did I not see that coming? What the hell did I do? Every single day I look at my phone, especially during the hours he normally calls.

My heart is screaming, "Call him! Talk to him!" My brain reasons and says, "Don't. He asked you not to. Respect his wishes even if it's eating you alive."

Pure agony. It's a good thing that I can isolate my personal life from my professional life. In the clinic, I block everything from my mind and focus on my patients a hundred percent. Driving home and being home is another story.

Finally, after 3 punishing months, I get the phone call I have been waiting for. It's evening; I'm alone in my room and sitting at my desk. It's still cold outside, and it gets even colder when I see the caller ID come across my phone.

I hold my breath, scared to answer. I wait for 3 more rings before I answer the call, my hands trembling. I hear him. "Hi ... it's me," followed by silence.

The voice—quiet, hesitant, devoid of warmth, and the long pause that followed told me everything. It's over.

It wasn't his usual "Hi, love." Or "Hi, sweetie." I can hear pain. I can hear defeat. Still, I want to make sure.

My heart is pounding and searing in pain as I ask, "What have you decided? I really need to know." Pools of tears are forming in my eyes. My breathing is shallow and short. I'm trying so hard not to scream.

He answers, "I love you but not enough to be with you. I can't do this to you or myself anymore. We need to let go and move on separately."

The searing pain in my heart only gets worst. Now it's ripping apart piece by piece. I lost him once before, and when we reconnected, we both thought this was for good. Now I'm losing him again, permanently. Miraculously, I hold it together until the phone call ends for the very last time.

It hurt tremendously that he so strongly felt that way and that there was nothing I could do to help him, that my success after years of working my tail off was something he could not handle.

I'll never forget the physical pain in my heart. It wasn't a mere figure of speech. It felt like a knife slashing through my heart; so intense that it even hurt to breathe.

It took me 2 years to recover from that pain, and although I am stronger and wiser, the memory of it still haunts me if I allow it to.

Unreciprocated Love

Have you ever felt like you gave of yourself unconditionally, heart and soul, but were not loved back? It's a gnawing, aching feeling of emptiness and sadness regardless of the circumstance—between families, friends, or lovers.

Loving unconditionally is also an act of vulnerability. You put it all out there. You open your heart and give of yourself completely.

Reciprocated, it's the best feeling in the world. When it's not, it's a pain you do not ever forget.

Veronica feels like her mother hates her for as long as she can remember. She is warm, loving and full of praise for others, but toward Veronica, aloof and cold. There are no warm hugs or encouragement growing up.

When I ask her about fond, loving memories, she tells me she can't recall any. She says that toward her siblings, she can, but not for herself, no matter how hard she tries. She has no recollections of being told "I love you" and dreams of the moment she'll hear "I'm sorry for all the pain I've caused you."

Years turned the pain into resentment, and the struggle continues to this day.

A Voice Unheard

"My words fell on deaf ears." It's one thing if the person truly didn't or couldn't hear, but when it's said because you were ignored or ridiculed, it's another issue altogether.

It becomes even more difficult to accept when you feel that your plea is urgent or important but of no value to a person you love.

I had been married for 14 months. My husband and I had just welcomed our firstborn son 2 months before. My life had been picture perfect to that point.

The problem began when I noticed that a woman frequently called our home in the evenings to speak to my husband, also a physician, for 'medical advice.' This was the same woman his secretary had told me was openly flirting with him whenever she would come for appointments.

He reassured me that there was nothing going on, yet the evening calls continued even for advice unrelated to the doctor/patient relationship, which worried me even more. Whenever I tried to talk to him about it, he'd quickly brush me off. I trusted his word, but her growing desire for his attention bothered me.

After putting my baby to sleep one evening, I approached him to voice my growing fear, knowing that she had another appointment scheduled with him the following day. What happened next was not something I ever expected.

First came the usual attempt to brush me off. When I persisted, he got angry, began to mock me and call me 'crazy and insecure.' When the tears of hurt and disbelief began, without warning, I was pummeled with fists meant for a punching bag; rapid fire, full force.

I still see that moment clearly in my mind. I'm sitting, cross-legged on our bed, with him standing by the edge, to my left. I'm crying and looking away, hurt because of the insults and look of disgust on his face.

Suddenly, I hear a loud whack and feel terrible pain on my left shoulder. Thinking that he lost his balance and tripped, I look up and see in disbelief that his hands are clenched into tight fists, his eyes wide and filled with rage, and he hits me again.

I scream and wail, immobilized by pain and shock, cowering in fear. The louder I cry, the faster and stronger the fists come down. It's raining punches now. At this point, I can no longer move my arm; it is as heavy as lead, and I realize I need to save myself.

Holding my arm secure, I muster the strength to jump up, run as fast as I could around him and lock myself in the bathroom where I crumple on the floor sobbing in stunned agony. This was the beginning of our end.

PUTTING THE PAST FAR BEHIND

I need to make one thing very clear. If any progress is to be made in helping yourself, you MUST be willing and able to put the past far behind you.

I didn't say forget. I'm saying *put it behind you*. If right from the start you say you can't or won't do this, neither I nor anyone else can help you.

Here's why this is critical:

For as long as you hold on to the past, the struggle to climb out will exponentially be more difficult. Why? Let me give you three valid reasons:

One, constantly living in all that pain, hurt, disappointment or unhappiness will only weigh you down.

Remember that whirlpool or quicksand analogy? Now add the 'weight' of each negative emotion you carry—that you refuse to let go. Now you're sinking faster and deeper.

How long are you going to hold on to the weight before you eventually drown?

The memory of that weight will always be there, but it's how we use it that makes a world of difference. I'm going to show you what I mean further on in this book.

The second valid reason why you must be willing to put the past behind you is that if you don't, you will always use this as your crutch or your excuse why you 'can't' move forward.

I cannot tell you how many of my clients do this, making recovery and improvement so difficult. "I can't because this happened to me before. I'm scared to try because he/she did this in the past."

It becomes a convenient excuse and gives them what they believe in their mind is a valid reason why they 'can't' make progress. In truth, they are only fooling themselves because once they let go, the journey to healing truly begins.

Third, your life will continue to manifest your thoughts. If in your mind you think, *I'm going to fail again. I'm going to get hurt. People always disappoint me. I can't seem to find happiness* — guess what you are subconsciously attracting into your life. If negative thoughts and emotions dominate, that is the same kind of energy you attract into your life.

How do I know? I've been there. Behold the power of the mind! Once a shift in that thinking is made, the changes that follow will amaze you.

Let me go through the steps I've taken in teaching my clients to put the past behind.

Facing the Pain Head On

As painful as it is to remember and almost relive the pain, it is crucial that we face it and look right into its eye. Ignoring it, pushing it aside, brushing it away, sweeping it under the rug—or worst, denying that it even existed—will not at all help to conquer it. You must see it for what it is and how deeply it affected you.

It is important to also understand the circumstances surrounding it—because there you will find valuable lessons.

What was your role in it? Be brutally honest with yourself. This is not the time to point fingers or beat yourself down either. It's merely the time to try to understand what brought about that pain in order to have some clarity as to why it happened.

There are countless ways we experience pain of all degrees. I have shared with you personal and painful moments of my life to help you understand this process.

Facing the pain from my past never was easy, but it was necessary because now I understand the 'why.'

I have been physically beaten more than once in a relationship I thought would last forever, leaving me with bruises on my body and my spirit, mocked and insulted; rejected by one I had loved for 8 years and betrayed by another.

The shock and heartbreak from the first two were the hardest to bear, but my love for my two children kept me fighting to pick up the shattered pieces and live again.

I took a step back and looked at who we were then, the surrounding circumstances, and how that affected us. I left judgment, blame, anger, hurt, and all other negative emotions aside to see things for what they were.

I realized it wasn't about me. They were in pain and turmoil too, in one way or another. They felt threatened, and their own life's experiences taught them to react the way they did, as mine taught me.

Who am I to judge right or wrong?

Recognizing How Pain Changed You

Every experience we go through in life, good or bad, changes us in some way.

My pain changed me. For one, it taught me to open my eyes beyond myself. I put myself in their shoes, knowing them the way I did. It couldn't have been easy for them either.

Life molded them into who they were, and if I allowed myself to see that, it made it less difficult for me to understand why they reacted to how they perceived the change.

Secondly, it gave me the opportunity to learn more about myself and be accepting of my weaknesses and strengths.

What change in me triggered the change in them? Was I disrespectful or cocky? Can I look at myself in the mirror and truthfully say my words or actions did not hurt them too? How did I change? Was there growth and success? Was there improvement? What did I learn? Was I true to myself, and can I be proud of what I did?

Lastly, the pain made me more cautious around men; 'gun-shy' if you will. I have not become bitter, angry, or condemning. I acknowledge my worth and am more careful now about who I open my heart to again.

I have come to realize that with or without someone in my life, I am now at peace and happy with myself.

Acknowledging That Things Cannot Be Changed

Oh, the what ifs!

When all hell first breaks loose, the mind doesn't think straight. Emotions are so high that speaking or behaving at the height of it is not the wisest. When the reality sets in, the questioning begins.

What did I do? What if I had done it this way? How could I not have seen it? How can I fix it? What if I do this, or that?

Sometimes we could have done something differently, and sometimes it would not have mattered in the first place. The point is, it's done. It happened. It cannot be erased and neither can time be reversed for a re-do.

The moment we realize that what happened cannot be changed and accept it, the sooner we can move forward.

I questioned myself at nauseum. There was a lot of self-blame. "I could have ... I shouldn't have ... Maybe if I didn't do that, this wouldn't have happened ..."

Reality sucks, but ALWAYS, there are lessons we learn. There were lessons we needed to learn, understand, and try our best to grow from. I couldn't change the way they thought or felt, but I could change mine.

That brings me to another important point.

Don't expect people to change either. Some people do; some people don't. But waiting, praying, hoping for them to change the way YOU want them to will only cause you frustration, aggravation, and disappointment if they are not willing or able to do so.

Remember this well: People are capable of change, but not everyone will be willing to change. If they did, it would have already been done.

What is important is changing the way you handle their resistance. Are you going to keep on fighting them like rams butting heads? Or are you going to accept that some things cannot be changed and work your way around that with as minimal stress to yourself as possible?

Your choice. What will it be?

Deciding Who Dominates: Your Past or You

Here's the crucial part. So we got hit hard and were knocked down. Now what? There are only two options here: stay down or get up. What will it be? "Will I wallow in the pain or will I dust off the broken shreds and stand again?"

I totally understand how incapacitating the pain can be. Just getting out of bed in the morning becomes an ordeal. Every breath hurts. Your mind is so heavily clouded that you can barely even think straight, let alone take care of yourself. Sleep eludes you, and when you finally do and wake up, reality hits that you were not in a bad dream but are living the nightmare again.

Yes, it happened. Yes, things cannot be changed. Yes, you are heavily wounded. Yes, it hurts like hell.

Now comes the most important question you should ask yourself. "Where do I go from here? Up or down?"

This was my 'aha' moment.

In 2008, I hit rock bottom. I was stuck in a job I was so unhappy in because I was overworked and undervalued, suffered from a ruptured blood vessel in my brain, lost my father—whom I adored—to cancer and also lost the love of my life.

Boom, boom, BOOM!

One after another, it all hit me within a matter of 2 months. I put on a brave face in front of my young children, but inside, I was falling apart. One Sunday, while they were away on a playdate, I remember calling out to God as I wailed in my room. "I can't bear this anymore. Please! Help me! Guide me!"

It was in that moment of darkest despair, after the sobbing subsided, that I realized I had a choice as to what happened next. I could remain in my misery, or I could stand and take the first step forward.

My move. My choice.

Taking Control of Your Future

No one can make you do what you don't want to do. The decision is yours. The driving force in either direction comes from you.

You and only you can change the course of your path.

People and circumstances can lift you up or drag you down, but you take that first step in the direction you choose.

I knew that pivotal moment in 2008 would set my course in a monumental way.

I chose to stand up and take forward steps.

I was afraid that if I spent any more time in the pit of darkness that surrounded me, the effort to climb out would be even harder, steeper, and darker with each passing day.

Being a single Mom, I had 2 young children who depended on me. For a moment, I imagined how their life would change if I weren't there for them, and that was enough to bring out the Mama

Bear in me. I had to fight harder than I ever have. Not only my own but our survival depended on it.

That switch in mindset and shifts I share with you in this book was my manual for survival.

CHAPTER 3
Understanding the power of pain and how you can embrace it

One of the most powerful sensations that exist is pain. By definition, it is "the physical feeling caused by disease, injury, or something that hurts the body" as well as a "mental or emotional suffering."

Every living creature that has the capacity to experience pain tries to escape from it or avoid it. Pain evokes fear, stress, sadness, and even desperation and despair.

WHY PAIN EXISTS AND ITS RELEVANCE

So, why does it exist? What is its purpose? What good does it do?

In my profession, I see pain in all its many facets: physical, emotional, and mental. I have seen pain move mountains as well as seen pain destroy life.

I have been so moved and inspired by people who experience pain so devastating and unimaginable yet emerge through the storm strong and at peace.

On the other hand, I have also witnessed how it can seem so insurmountable to some that they lose hope, give up and stop living.

My understanding of pain has evolved over the years. I once thought of it as a punishment, a cruel joke, a terrible stroke of luck.

That view has since evolved tremendously. Life's experiences have taught me to now see pain in a different light and learn to accept and embrace it when it happens.

Yes, it still exists. There is no escaping pain. But understanding it made the difference. That switch changed my life.

Let me share my insights with you.

Life's Greatest Lesson

Experiencing pain yourself is so different from learning about it from the lives and experiences of others.

Have you ever read or heard about someone else's tragedy or misfortune and thought to yourself, *I can't imagine going through that; thank goodness that's not me?* You may have continued to learn about how that person overcame his/her trial and admired them for that, but then, in time, the story fades.

Pain does not come into our lives as a punishment, or because there is a sadistic Higher Being out there who wants us to suffer for no reason whatsoever.

I believe everything in life has a reason for being or happening. Every experience molds us. We do not emerge the same person. Something changes—for better or worse. There is either growth or regression/stagnation. Each event presents us with an opportunity to do so.

I have clients who have gone through unbelievable pain, like the death of a child or a lifelong condition either themselves or someone in their family (like cancer, a congenital disability, debilitating illness or catastrophic accident/circumstance) that leaves one incapacitated.

After the initial shock and pain, one thing that stands out to me most is that in time, many of them tell me of how they learned something good.

Let me give you a few examples: "It taught me to appreciate the little things in life ... My son taught me how it is to love unconditionally ... It brought us together as a family ... How she fights to survive teaches me courage and strength every day."

Of course, there are some who choose not to try to recover and shut themselves off from the world, but those who do emerge with greater insight and more positive outlook.

A Stamp in Our Memory

The pain we experience is never forgotten, but it is our choice how to handle or use that memory.

Looking back now at the most difficult times of my life, I realize how much I have learned and grown in the process; lessons I will never forget because that was MY journey and MY fight to live.

I remember the despair and pain as much as I remember the internal shifts that made each day more bearable.

I remember the people who were with me; the heaven-sent angels who helped me keep my head above water.

I remember feeling the strength build within me as I realized I had more days of smiles than tears.

Yes, the memory is painful, but I choose to focus on the wonderful outcome. A warrior was born, and I survived.

A Lifetime Reminder

When a similar scenario presents itself, remembering the pain you had gone through previously will hopefully arm you with the ammunition to conquer the pain you are facing again.

"I've been down this path before. Do I deal with it differently or will I choose the same method? Do I resign myself or do I find a better solution and work hard on it?"

Sometimes, life throws you a hurdle that seems all too familiar. Maybe it's because there is a lesson we have yet to master, or because you are stronger and better able to handle it.

I was in an abusive relationship in the past. I remember the shock of being pummeled for the first time because the eyes I saw behind the face were not of the person I loved. They were terrifying, almost demonic and looked possessed, so dark and spewing with rage.

There was so much pain from the punches, but even more pain realizing that the man I loved was the person inflicting the brutal blows. The third and final time was the worse because my 4½-year-old son witnessed it and tried to protect me. I also happened to be pregnant with my daughter. I still see that moment clearly in my mind.

I'm in the master bedroom, and the blows are coming at me again after an argument. I'm flailing my arms and screaming. I'm about to be dragged off the bed by my feet and claw at the bedsheets to keep from falling on my head. I manage to kick both feet lose and scramble to stand, staring once again at demonic eyes burning with rage.

In that moment, I hear "Mommy!!!" from the next room.

My son who had been sick and just fell asleep yells for me, frightened by the noise. I run to him, and his father follows to continue the punches. I scream and am knocked forward to the bed.

My son's eyes widen in sheer horror, and he starts to cry himself. He immediately jumps forward, straddling my lap, one little arm around my neck and the other outstretched to protect me as he yells, "Please stop, Dad! No!!! Don't hurt Mommy! No!!! Please stop!"

The blows did not stop, now combined with kicks aimed at my shoulders and back as I cradled and protected my son; kicks that flung my son and me apart with the brute force. Once again, my little boy jumps on my lap and begs his father to stop. This went on for what seemed like an eternity. Over and over again.

This is the moment when survival instinct kicks in. He can hurt me but over my dead body will he hurt my son.

I remember the animalistic scream that came from me as I grabbed my son, ran as fast as I could back to the master bedroom where I thankfully managed to lock the door. I called for help, and my brother immediately came to my aid.

It took a week for us to come home. That was the moment my marriage had died for good.

It was one thing to receive the blows, but this time, my little boy was involved, and that was the point of no return for me. When a man is so overpowered by rage that even a 4-year-old son shielding his mother and begging him to stop doesn't snap him out of it, you know in your heart you can't allow this to go on.

I freed myself from that relationship and vowed never to let that happen again.

Since then, any moment of conflict from anyone puts me on high alert to how the person reacts when angry. The eyes tell me everything. The ability to dissipate the emotion is what I study. How they behave after gives me the answers I need to know and has saved me from another relationship of pain.

THE ANSWER TO "WHY ME?"

How many times have you asked yourself that question when faced with pain?

I have. Many times before. At least I used to. It may not necessarily be said that way, but the thought or emotion is there.

"Really? Again? Unbelievable!"

"This is so unfair. Why can't I get a break?"

"How do others get to be so lucky? What's wrong with me?"

Life has a funny way of teaching us lessons. Many times, when we are deep in the trenches of our trials, it truly seems like nothing good or helpful can possibly come from what we go through.

How many times have you ever looked back, months or years later, and realized, "Oh, NOW I see why"? How many times have you realized that what seemed like the biggest disappointment was actually a blessing in disguise? How many times have you emerged wiser or stronger from a 'mistake' from the past?

"Why me?"

Here's what I've come to realize for myself:

No Two Lives Are Identical

No two circumstances are the same. We each go through our own unique battles.

No two lives are exactly the same, even as identical twins. Therefore, each experience is unique. You can learn how someone dealt with a crisis, but the full impact is only known when personally experienced.

There is a deeper understanding that comes from going through the process yourself.

Pain is an Opportunity to Find the Strength You Never Knew Existed

Sometimes the moments of greatest strength and resilience happen when you feel like you have no other option left and value what you want badly enough.

It's March 2008. I'm mourning the loss of my father, alone, and having excruciating headaches from my brain surgery. I'm sitting in bed, looking out the window with a blank stare.

It's a sunny Sunday afternoon, and there's a gentle breeze, but everything seems so dead and dark. So is the room, as if everything I see is covered in a dull cloud of grey. I have no desire to move. Even breathing and thinking is an effort.

I'm like a vehicle with an empty tank of gas— capable of movement but with nothing more to go on.

In that moment, I realize that I have a very important decision to make: move or die. I'm so exhausted that the easier choice for me is to give up.

However, two young children who I love with all my heart and call me Mama depend on me. I could not bear the thought of the agony they would go through if they lost me, so I chose to fight.

The day I made that choice was my turning point. I was fighting not only for myself but them, and there was no way I was going to put them through hell.

Just when I thought I had no willpower left in me, I dove into prayer, shifted my focus and mindset, found strength in the love of my children and fought for my life. Survival mode kicked in, and with that, the courage and determination to keep pushing ahead.

There is Always a Valuable Lesson Learned

The most valuable and unforgettable lessons learned are those you experience yourself with all its ups and downs.

I never forgot that pain and never forgot the struggle, but that journey taught me so much about myself and life in general.

I learned how strong I could be, how fierce I could fight, how powerful a positive mindset can be. I learned who my true friends were and appreciated them more.

I learned that I could turn my life around if I wanted something bad enough. I learned that I needed to be honest with myself and courageous about change if I wanted to be happy in life.

So you see, life didn't hand me just lemons during the dark times. I walked away a warrior, armed with powerful lessons that will help me conquer whatever else comes my way.

IT'S NOT ABOUT YOU

Realizing this was one of the most liberating, life-changing moments I've ever had. All those years of feeling like I was short-changed in life, a victim, unworthy and not good enough evaporated. It felt like decades of suffocating, heavy sadness, guilt, shame and disappointment were lifted off my heart and shoulders.

What helped me come to that realization? I opened my mind and understood what I'm going to share with you right now.

It's Not a War Against You

Pain and hardship do not happen because the world and humanity are sadistic. It's a lesson you must learn to move forward.

There is no personal vendetta against you. Life will always have its highs and lows. One side cannot exist without the other. In the same light, everything that happens has a purpose.

We hear "It happened by accident" or "What a coincidence that was," as if things happen randomly with no rhyme or reason.

Imagine the chaos in this world if that were actually true. We are happy and excited when things go the way we want, but sometimes quick to complain or feel oppressed if they don't. It will not always be a bed of roses, and <u>it's not because of you</u>.

There is a lesson to learn from every experience. Realize too that the harder the lesson, the more it is remembered, and the sweeter the success.

In the beginning, I frequently used to question why. "Why me? Why is life so hard? Why does it have to be this way? Why can't I seem to get a break?" With lessons learned comes growth, and I am wiser because of it.

The only question I ask now is, "What am I supposed to learn from this?" and what a difference that viewpoint makes.

<u>How People React is a Reflection of Their Lives and Experiences</u>

How people react to you or toward you is a reflection of what they have gone through in their lives and how they have learned to deal with it. No one starts their day with the sole intention to make you miserable.

My mentor opened my eyes to this perspective, and what a difference it has made in my life. It all boils down to a very important starting point: it's not about me.

The love of my life for 8 years did not walk away because of something I did. I cannot tell you how many years I have agonized over that, trying to find the answer to that heartbreaking 'why.'

"What did I do? What could I have done differently?" Then we start to attack ourselves. "Am I not good enough? Am I no longer desirable? Is it because I am older or gained weight? Did I nag? Did I say something wrong?" Nothing made sense to me then. I thought everything was great and as good as it could be, which is why his choice to walk away shattered me.

A year ago, I learned he got married, and I have to admit it stung. I had a good talk with my mentor, no longer wanting to feel the pain and self-doubt all over again.

Seeing where the conversation was heading, he stopped me in my tracks and said, "He left the relationship because HE was not capable of handling the perceived threat your success brought on his masculinity. There was nothing you could have done."

Kaboom!

I saw the light and how liberating that was! I used that perspective to understand other traumatic events in my life, and all the years of self-doubt or feeling like a victim faded away.

Freeing Yourself From the Chains of Victimhood

Once you realize that it's not about you, it frees you from feeling like people, life, or the world itself are out to get you/destroy you.

Let me give you an example: being physically abused in the past.

Every circumstance that surrounded those beatings had something to do with loss of control. Early in that relationship, I was a naive 24-year-old girlfriend who did everything I was told. I was eager to please, so I followed what he wanted and waited on his opinion before taking action.

Inevitably, I began to develop opinions of my own as a wife, especially when I realized that my ideas would have saved us both time, money, and aggravation.

This was when the problem started. The more I questioned his way and offered my opinion, the more conflict grew. That's when the mocking and insults began. He was used to being followed without resistance.

The day I held my ground was the very first time I was met with a fury of rapid-fire fist blows. Physical abuse should never be tolerated, yet I blamed myself.

"I shouldn't have spoken up. I should have just followed. It's my fault because I made him so angry. I shouldn't have gotten so emotional and raised my voice."

I kept this from my family because I was afraid of what they would say. Not even my closest friends knew.

I suffered in silence.

In my mind, I was another victim of physical abuse and had to bear it, partly blaming myself for triggering that anger.

Looking back at this years after, I realized again that it wasn't about me. I can't apologize for my growing independence. I wasn't weak, helpless, or incapable of thinking or acting on my own—as I was made to believe.

I was evolving as a person; improving. He didn't suddenly wake up one day and think, *I'm going to start punching and kicking my wife from now on.* Somehow, sometime, somewhere in his past, he learned to react this way when he felt threatened or lost control.

It wasn't about a plot to hurt me for no reason. It wasn't even about me.

I have no anger, bitterness and do not walk with wounds. We are friends today, I care about him and I will always wish him the best. We can speak to each other without animosity and even celebrate our kids' special events together.

I'm in a good place now, and so is he, *separately.*

Yes, the lessons were very painful, but we both have come a long way individually.

CHAPTER 4
Acknowledging your birthright and claiming it

How fiercely do you protect something that's rightfully yours?

Let's say a thief steps inside your home and wants to strip it bare of everything you own. What are you going to do? What about if the intruder now gets into your garage and intends to drive away with your car—will you let that person get away with it?

Now let's say that thief now wants to hurt you or take a loved one away that moment. How ferociously will you fight to save yourself and the people you care about? With every ounce of power you have, right?

Hold that thought for a moment.

What if I told you that you were born to succeed and born to greatness? Would you let anyone or anything rob you of that birthright? Would you give up your power to live the life you desire if it was yours to own from the moment of your conception?

Let's break that down and start from the very beginning.

BORN TO SUCCEED

You Survived Against the Odds

You were conceived after 1 sperm out of 50 to 500 million others managed to survive to fertilize an ovum within your mother. Even with that success, your mother had a 15 to 20% chance of miscarriage before she even knew she was pregnant.

Around 20 out of 1000 pregnancies do not make it to the uterus to continue with the progression to your birth.

Of those that do, other complications could have happened, resulting in death, such as severe infections, very premature birth, significant abnormalities in the development of the fetus, and problems with the birth itself.

Yet, you survived.

Yes, YOU!

You were not miscarried or aborted. You went through a very intricate and delicate process of cell growth to become uniquely you.

Your birth, in itself, was your very first success.

You Were Born Fearless

Nothing could stop you when you were a toddler. You were not afraid to try. You were a daredevil. You likely had a parent or caregiver running after you, telling you to stop or trying to correct you, but that didn't stop you from trying. You knew no fear.

I remember my children when they were toddlers. They were like wind-up toys with boundless energy. They overflowed with curiosity and eagerness to try anything they were interested in.

Unless it involved something that I believed would truly hurt them, like electrical sockets, I let them be.

I remember the look on their faces when they fell. Stunned, but they'd still get up and carry on, maybe with just a little more caution. If they fell hard, yes, they'd cry, but nothing that a kiss on the spot from me can't comfort. The cry was short-lived, then off they'd go again.

The point is, unless someone followed you around, telling you to stop or scolding you for trying something they thought was not good for you, you knew no fear.

The sky was your limit.

You Were Born Resilient

The very first time you succeeded was when you overcame the odds and were born. So many things could have gone wrong, as I had mentioned, but you made it.

After you were born, you had the will to survive.

Think about it. No one comes into this world and declares, "I want to die."

The power of the human will should never be underestimated, even in the tiniest infant.

In my career as a pediatrician and intensive care doctor, I have watched in awe countless babies and children beat the odds and live. Unless there was a force/disease/abnormality greater than what their bodies could handle, believe me, they fought for life.

I'll never forget Luke, a 15-year-old kid who came into the intensive care unit after being hit by a train. He got off the wrong side and was thrown at least 15 ft. away, hitting his head on impact.

He suffered from a severe case of traumatic brain injury and was in a coma. After his heart stopped the third time, his parents tearfully signed a 'do not resuscitate' order. This meant that if his heart stopped again, we would not try to bring him back because each time it did injured his brain even more.

Well, guess what, he stunned us all.

Not only did his heart continue to beat strong, but he lived to tell me how each time he 'went to heaven,' his grandfather who he was very close to told him to go back because it wasn't his time yet. He is one of many miracles of survival.

Never underestimate the power of the human will.

BORN TO GREATNESS

Your Birth Was No Mistake

You are not an accident. You are purposely placed on earth for a reason. Nature has a way of taking care of itself. If you were too weak or deformed, you would have naturally aborted.

According to infertility specialists, the chances of any woman being able to conceive at any given month is only about 1:7. Of that, there is a 15–20% chance of abortion for a number of reasons, sometimes even before the woman finds out she is pregnant.

You developed into a viable human being and were born against the odds.

Your birth was not an error. In fact, it was a story of triumph in itself.

Look around you.

There are countless stories of people who, despite what life throws at them, emerge victorious.

Why? Because we all have it in us.

The difference? Because they were determined, believed in their mind and heart that they could, and were unshakable in their will to keep on going.

I see it often enough in all my years of practice. Tiny ones who fight for their lives with unimaginable spunk and will and grow up to shine as bright, if not brighter than all the rest.

In my moments of emotional fatigue, I think of them for inspiration to keep moving forward. What incredible reminders they are of how great life can be!

You Play a Valuable Role in This World

You are born to fulfill a purpose in this world: to learn lessons and to be a lesson for others as well. Don't let your time go to waste.

As a physician, I have had the joy and honor of witnessing the beauty of human life from birth to death. Even through significant illness or lifelong disability, I have seen the roles each person plays in this world.

Whereas I once felt sorry for a family if their child was born with a problem that has a lifelong sentence, I now see with my own eyes what unconditional love is all about. I cannot tell you how many times these families tell me what a blessing that child is in their lives, even in their fragile existence.

They teach patience, show love so innocent and pure. Families learn to appreciate the simplest things in life, like a good day without pain, or a word uttered, a smile and loving hug, the dedication of their doctors, to name a few. The same goes for families dealing with older individuals.

Somehow, in some very special way, there is a profound and heartfelt role we all play in this world.

You Have the Ability to Achieve Anything You Want

Hellen Keller is an excellent example. She became deaf and blind as a baby—before she even learned to speak—but never gave up. She went on to become an author, political activist, lecturer and the first deaf/blind person to earn a Bachelor of Arts degree.

She easily could have but made no excuses. She set her mind on what she wanted, went for it with tenacity and never gave up.

The day my life turned around was the day I eliminated the words 'I can't,' 'It's too hard,' and 'maybe' from my vocabulary for myself.

If I wanted something bad enough, like to pull out of my misery and not only survive but thrive, I realized that there could be no doubt in my mind. I set one small goal for each day and made sure I got that ONE simple task done.

Baby steps. That's how to begin.

In time, the stride gets bigger and bolder. Confidence grows. Before you know it, you've done it, and boy what an incredible feeling that is!

CLAIMING WHAT IS RIGHTFULLY YOURS

Owning Your Uniqueness

There's nobody else in the world like you, and you are in this world for a purpose.

Embrace all you are, imperfections and weaknesses included. Why? Because there are two sides to a spectrum; life's balance.

You are beautiful in your own way and have your own strengths. Stop trying to compare yourself to someone else.

Own who you are and what you are here for.

Comparing yourself to someone else does you no justice. I see this often enough with my clients.

"I wish I was like her." "Why can't I be as good as him?" "Why can't my life be as easy as theirs?"

When this is the mentality, the focus becomes the LACK OF whatever that is: lack of love, money, happiness, luck, you name it. It leaves you feeling inadequate and mostly sorry for yourself.

Carrie is in her mid-20s and a mother of 2 rambunctious kids. She frequently comes in close to tears because her little boys are 'out of control,' her house is a mess, and she feels inadequate as a mom and wife. She compares herself to her friends "who have it together so well."

She wants help because she senses that her stress levels are affecting her relationship with her husband. She fears that he sees her as incapable of much responsibility and will begin to lose interest in her as a wife.

"He comes home to a madhouse, and I see the look on his face. He's tired himself, and I can't even keep a decent home for him to come home to at the end of the day. The kids are usually crying, haven't had their baths, dinner is late, toys are all over the house, a pile of laundry undone, and I look like I had been through a windstorm. He just lets out a sigh and gives me a peck on my cheek. He doesn't say much, but the look in his eyes is one of exasperation. Our level of intimacy has declined, and it's all my fault! I can't handle anything!"

Little by little, we focused on the qualities she did have instead of what she perceived she didn't. I remember her trembling, and the 'deer-in-the-headlights' look on her face when I advised her on how we would begin, starting off with her children.

I held her hands and looked into her eyes amidst the chaos of one child having a flailing meltdown on the floor and the other climbing on the table with the intent to jump off.

We took quiet control of the situation, and she worked on that at home consistently. Then came another task which she practiced on.

The woman who walked into my office a few months down the road was a far cry from the person I first met.

She looked absolutely gorgeous in her colorful spring dress, her hair down with soft waves framing her face, stood and walked taller, had a big smile on her face and sparkle in her blue eyes. Gone were the leggings; crumpled, stained shirt; messy pony-tail; and flip-flops.

What triggered it? She began to believe in herself, did not let her shortcomings weigh her down and owned her worth.

Owning Your Strength

You have it in you. It exists.

It may have been dampened by misfortunes, hardships, or failures, but it remains in you. You've heard of people rise above tremendous adversities that many would have given up on.

How did they do it? They found and owned their strength, and that gave them the drive to push through and succeed.

My colleague's 22-year-old daughter Karla was involved in a freak accident. She fell from a ledge and landed on her back 10 ft. below when her friend accidentally tripped and lunged toward her.

She sustained a spinal injury and was nearly completely paralyzed below her waist. We all feared the worst because her best response was a very weak wiggle of her toe on one foot.

The most important factors this young lady had were tenacious determination and a fighting spirit. She beat the odds and is now able to walk unassisted because she never gave up trying.

Claiming Your Birthright

Once again, I ask you:

How fiercely do you protect something valuable to you that you were gifted since the day you were born? You guard it with your life, don't you?

What would you do if someone tried to take it away from you, or tell you that you cannot have something that belongs to you? You'd fight for it, right?

If your birthright is to be uniquely great, strong and achieve anything you set your mind to, what's stopping you from claiming that?

It's rightfully yours. Own it. Claim it.

Fight for it!

CHAPTER 5

Recognizing and finding solutions to your roadblocks

I f you are born to greatness and born to succeed but find yourself far from where you want to be, it goes without saying that something in your life is keeping you from getting there. These obstacles could be people, bad experiences from past events, or perceived misfortunes, to name a few.

But do you know what the biggest obstacle of all is? Take a guess.

The biggest obstacle is YOU.

Somewhere, somehow, sometime in the past ... when trials in life made you doubt your birthright ... you lost your fearless spunk along with it.

It's crucial that you face your roadblocks again because it is only in understanding how they've held you down can you begin your fight to overcome them and win.

FACING THE DEMONS

Unworthiness

Seeing no value in yourself.

"I don't deserve it. I'm not appreciated or loved."

There are different ways we can feel unworthy.

It may be tied to other negative emotions such as guilt and shame. "I did something wrong; therefore, I'm not worthy of something good" or "I hurt a lot of people; therefore, I don't deserve happiness."

It can also exist alone, brought about by feeling unloved or unappreciated.

Remember Joe? All his life, he felt like he was not good enough for his parents, no matter how hard he tried to please them. He felt unappreciated, which, after years, turned into the belief that he was 'a waste of space' and not worthy of anything good.

Guilt

"I made mistakes in the past/ I've hurt people/ I haven't been honest.   This is why my life sucks now."

For many years, I was ridden with guilt about not being able to give my children an intact family life I always dreamed for them. They were too young and confused, not knowing why their father and I parted ways.

My son would cry every time his dad would leave after visiting, and I'd sit in his bed, comfort him and hold his hand until he fell asleep. He suddenly had to grow up and felt like he was the 'man of the house' at age 7, so protective of me. My daughter didn't even get to have a memory of a complete family.

I was sad for their father, missing out on their little milestones. I felt guilty that we failed them, our children. Even if I knew it was for the best, I still felt guilty for the sadness it caused many people.

I also felt guilty finding love elsewhere because I knew in my heart that what my kids wished for was that their father and I would reconcile. They were too young to understand the magnitude of why we divorced, and their pain became a tremendous load of guilt I bore for many years.

It convinced me that I would not be able to find true love and happiness with another man as 'punishment' for other people's pain.

Shame

"I've failed too many times. I'm not good enough. What will people think of me if I don't succeed again? What do they think of me now?"

Failure and defeat sure have a way of eroding into our confidence and planting seeds of shame and/or regret, coupled with fear and insecurity.

At some point in our lives, we thought we were invincible, daring to try whatever we thought was going to be fun or interesting. Life has a way of teaching us lessons, which either 'make' or 'break' a person.

Of all my 'failures' in my life, I considered the dissolution of my marriage as one of the biggest.

I had dreamed of a 'till death do us part' and was certain I married the right man for me. As the events unfolded, I questioned myself constantly.

"What did I do? Was I wrong? How did I not see this coming? How did it get this bad?"

I come from a family of devout Roman Catholics. I am the only one whose marriage failed. Regardless of the grave circumstances and fear for my life, I committed a sin.

I'll never forget my brother-in-law telling me just a month after my father died how sorry he was for me. "You'll never see your dad again in heaven because you're living in sin and going to hell." Not that I believed that for a second, but I still lived in shame.

I failed my children, my family, and myself.

Hopelessness

"I give up because I don't think there's anything I can do. I'm lost and tired."

Hopelessness, to me, is like drowning.

You put up a fight in the beginning—fighting for your survival. You may come up to the surface for life-saving oxygen, but when you spend more time underwater, eventually you tire and do not have the strength to keep your head above water.

My deepest sense of hopelessness was that period in the winter of 2008.

It's January, to be exact. I am in a small remote town of Maryland with no family or relatives nearby. My father is dying from cancer. I am imprisoned by a contract I cannot break in a job where I am not treated nor compensated fairly; not allowed to leave to see my father; excruciating headaches plague me every day; the love of my life is gone, and I am all alone with my children, struggling to survive and keep sane.

The evening of the 24th, as I stand to go to bed at 11:30 p.m., I am overcome with pain so sudden and severe that it knocks me off my feet. I feel as if someone took a sword and slashed open the back of my nape.

Fear overcomes me. I am alone with 2 young children. I think about calling 911 for a brief moment but am hesitant to leave my kids behind, not knowing who else to ask for help.

I take care of myself as best as I can, taking medication for my blood pressure that was very high and my migraine tablet. I fall asleep as I contemplate what to do next, waiting for the pain to subside. My sleep is restless because the pain doesn't go away.

I call my boss at 6 a.m., saying I need to see my doctor, but he brushes me off and insists I have to come to work. I get my children off to school and drag myself to the clinic, barely able to function from the pain. Thankfully, the secretaries intervene on my behalf after I struggle for an hour, defy my boss and send me off to see my doctor.

Fast forward four hours later, I am being airlifted to the University of Maryland hospital for blood in my brain. An undetected aneurysm had ruptured, and every minute I continued to bleed could be catastrophic or even fatal. Less than 24 hours later, I am scheduled for emergency brain surgery. I am told by my neurosurgeon that I may lose my ability to speak, move the right side of my body, and possibly not survive the surgery. If I did survive, there was a chance I could have a debilitating or fatal stroke within the first two weeks.

Less than a month later, my father passes away, and with him went a huge piece of heart. March comes along, and I'm struggling to carry on. I continue to have debilitating headaches (a side effect of brain surgery); I'm mourning my father terribly; I am back working earlier than I should because I have bills to pay; I'm all alone and caring for my children.

It is a struggle on all dimensions: physically, mentally, emotionally, spiritually. I feel broken, stuck and tired with no obvious end in sight. I keep it together around my children but sob each night, muffling my cries with my pillow.

I hit rock bottom.

It feels like I'm drowning and am so tired that I think about giving up.

FIGHTING AGAINST APATHY

Recognizing Your Triggers That Breed Apathy

What demon affects you most? Unless you acknowledge it and face it head on, there can be no growth.

Why? Because to overcome this, you have to dig deep into the core of the pain and understand its power over you before you can fight against it.

Recognizing the triggers that brought me so close to apathy was painful. It was like re-opening old wounds that never really healed. It was waking up emotions that I tried so hard to ignore and bury.

I realized, though, that I could never run away from them. They would always be there, ingrained in my memory.

If I wanted to rise above it, I had to face it head on, recognize how it affected my life and decide how I was going to deal with it.

Committing to Yourself

No one can do this for you if you are not willing to put in the effort.

You can have all the advice in the world, but if you do not practice daily what it takes to succeed, it's not going to happen.

No matter how much people try to help you—whether it's hours spent in counseling, encouragement from family and loved ones, months in a support group—the most important factor to success is your commitment to yourself.

How much do you want things to change? How important is change to you? How determined are you to succeed?

When I hit rock bottom, it got to the point where I felt like it had turned into a 'do or die' situation. Some family and friends were sympathetic and patiently listened to my grief. I felt comfort in that moment, but that quickly dissipated once the conversation ended.

All too quickly, I was back to feeling like I was sinking deeper in quicksand. Others didn't seem to care either because they were tired of me being that way or maybe even thought I deserved it.

The longer it lasted, the more desolate I felt. The day came when it felt like "there's no one left but me."

It was in that moment of deep and dark despair when I knew I had to make a choice.

Fight or drown.

I chose to commit to my children and myself and give the fight of my life.

Now I'm not a very religious person, but I hung on to my faith as my one remaining lifeline. I was so broken, drained and lost, desperate to see even a glimmer of light and hope.

I then spent hours in quiet meditation. I surrendered myself to the God I knew. No memorized or recited prayers. All I asked for was guidance and strength.

I focused on one positive thing each day just to get through, even something as simple as not having to answer patients' calls that night or soaking in the tub after the kids went to bed.

I committed to taking care of myself and getting braver each day.

Learning the 5 Secrets to Reclaiming Your Power and Living It

Here is my lifeline, my saving grace:

Whenever I become aware that a trigger is beginning to rear its ugly head and threatening to send me down a slippery spiral again, I remind myself of my secrets and practice them.

I'm going to go through each step with you in the following chapters. They will become your greatest weapons to fight apathy, conquer your demons and become the best version of you.

CHAPTER 6
#1 Engage with fearless honesty

FINDING YOUR VOICE

We were born very vocal.

We were loud and did not hold back when we wanted something. We spoke our minds with no filters.

"Out of the mouth of babes." We said what we were thinking and did not hold back or worry.

Society, over time, muted us.

"Keep quiet. I don't want to hear another word from you. That's not a nice thing to say. Don't say that, or he/she'll get upset. That's wrong. You take back what you said right now."

We need to peel back the layers of tape covering our mouths and speak up as fearlessly as we did when we were little—respectfully.

Speak what you truly feel in your heart, in your own voice and your own words. Not what anyone else expects or wants you to say.

You see, the problem that happens when we don't is that somewhere down the line, something's going to eventually break.

In time, resentment rears its menacing head, and relationships start to fall apart.

SPEAK WITH HONESTY

By age 3, most children know how to distort the truth, and by age 6, lie a few times a day. How did they learn? By observing their parents or caregivers. Around 60% of adults can typically tell 2–3 lies over a 10-minute conversation.

So WHY do we lie?

We learned growing up that when we speak the truth, someone at some point causes us pain in the form of guilt, shame, fear, rejection, or loss.

Every person wants love, comfort, and security. We twist, withhold, or color our truth when we feel it isn't safe to be honest.

But dishonesty comes with consequences.

When we are not honest, we are living in an alternate reality that becomes more complicated and stressful. At some point, we can't even keep track of who we told what.

I was taught strict obedience growing up. If you stray, you pay the price, so I became a follower. Many of my choices were to please people and avoid conflict.

I was scared of my mother's wrath. I was afraid to displease my father. I was worried about upsetting people if I said what I truly felt or disagreed to do what they wanted; about being labeled the black sheep, the troublemaker, the disappointment. I was afraid to speak up.

You see, dishonesty comes in two ways: altering the truth or withholding it. Either way leads to stress, unhappiness, and resentment. Eventually, one or all sentiments will reach boiling point and explode, guaranteed, and it's not going to be pretty.

Look at it this way too: If you never speak up, and the day comes when 'all hell breaks loose,' the other party involved will very likely say, "Where the heck did that come from? I didn't see this coming! Why didn't you say so in the first place?"

Understand this well: You can't make everyone happy. Whichever way you choose, someone is bound to be displeased. When you go against what fully resonates with you and what you truly desire, guess what, that someone is going to be you. In time, regret and/or resentment are going to surface. It's only going to be a matter of time.

When you learn to engage with fearless honesty consistently, you'll be more at peace, less stressed and able to carry out your day with confidence and simplicity.

No need to hide or be afraid to express your desire.

No more little lies just to make everyone else happy.

Wake up every morning confident. Go to sleep each night with peace of mind.

Start by creating an environment where people in your life feel safe telling the truth and be vulnerable without being judged, criticized, or attacked. Strengthening your muscles of compassion will silence your own fear.

Be the person you would love to have in your life.

If you want people to be trusting and honest with you, be honest and trustworthy *first*. Don't expect anyone to do what you're not willing to do yourself.

Think about this: When was the last time someone felt safe to open up to you without feeling judged or criticized?

Remember: we attract what we manifest.

If you manifest honesty, understanding, and compassion, *that* is what you will be attracting into your life as well. Imagine the difference it would make!

I made a conscious effort to practice this as I raised my children. I didn't want them to ever be fearful of expressing their choices, desires, and dreams with me. Neither did I want them to be afraid of talking to me about mistakes, heartaches, and failures.

I would always say, "What is it you want? Tell me what you are thinking. How do you feel you should go about this? What do you want to do? Whatever you decide, I'm going to support you."

It was important for me to also acknowledge my own shortcomings to them. I apologized when I was wrong or caused them hurt. I was honest and sincere, and it meant the world to them.

"I said hurtful things in anger, and I'm sorry that caused you pain."

"I understand how you feel, and I'm sorry that what I did or how I reacted hurt you."

I tried my best to be the person I would love to have in my life. I made mistakes, but I always worked toward improvement.

Now, my relationship with my kids is as wonderful as it can get. There is no fear or judgment between us. Honesty, love, and compassion thrive.

CHAPTER 7
#2 Own your worth

Those development of our self-worth starts in our childhood.

Remember, you were born to succeed; fearless, resilient, relentless. You were born to greatness.

Depending on the people, environment, and experiences in your life, that belief was either nurtured and sharpened, or wounded and shattered. You learned to either believe in yourself or lose faith and confidence. Your dominant belief strongly influenced whether you blossomed or wilted.

Here's something very important I want you to understand and realize: when our emotional needs of affection, acceptance, approval, and praise from those who raised us were not provided, human nature will tend to believe we are not worthy of them.

Without affection and acceptance, it's easy to feel unloved, not good enough, or not deserving of it.

UNDERSTANDING THE POWER OF THE SUBCONSCIOUS MIND

Let me tell you something very interesting about the human mind.

We have the conscious mind and the unconscious mind. What's important to know is that the subconscious mind is more powerful than the conscious mind.

Our subconscious mind controls around 90% of our thoughts. Therefore, we live our lives based on our subconscious thoughts.

Think about that for a moment.

We are what we think, even if we don't say it out loud.

If 90% of the time you think that you're unworthy of love, affection, and praise, then unconsciously, you may start to ACT on that belief.

Your subconscious mind protects your core beliefs. Whenever you try to change those beliefs, the subconscious mind will, therefore, try to resist the change.

Let me give you an example:

If you say you want to be happy and successful, but your subconscious mind tells you, "You're a miserable failure ..."—guess what wins? Quite powerful, right?

There is a constant tug of war, a struggle, an internal fight that never seems to end.

Unless you understand how your self-sabotaging core beliefs came to be *by no fault of your own*, there won't be an improvement.

Once the shift is made, and you learn to embrace your worth, be prepared to live in your magnificence.

Life has a funny way of clouding your vision if you misinterpret the challenges it presents for growth as unfortunate strokes of luck.

Before I learned to own my worth, my self-sabotaging thoughts made me believe I wasn't smart, strong, or good enough. My self-esteem was so low, and I began to feel so undesirable toward the end of my marriage that it actually surprised me when a person would compliment me.

I doubted and second-guessed myself so much.

"I don't know if I can do this. I'm not sure I have what it takes. What am I doing here? Will I be an embarrassment? Am I good and smart enough to go through this?"

These were the questions and fears I faced when I was going through my fellowship in Pediatric Critical Care. I was dealing with life and death situations every day. It was a very stressful and demanding 3 years of intense training.

My marriage had just fallen apart by the beginning of my second year in training; I was alone with 2 very young children, barely making ends meet financially, and was constantly exhausted by the demands of my job and being a single mother.

Life seemed to me then like a constant struggle. I wondered why nothing came easy to me, why everything seemed like it took so much effort to achieve. I wondered why the lives of others seemed smooth and easy compared to mine.

Looking back, I now understand why. I did not recognize my worth and was constantly filled with doubt. In my subconscious mind, I was unlucky, inferior and undesirable. No wonder it felt like I was always climbing a mountain!

HOW BADLY DO YOU WANT IT?

In the year 2008 when I hit rock bottom, the question I had to answer for myself was, "How badly do I want things to change?"

I realized that if I truly wanted my life to improve, I had to dust myself off from the pain of the past, focus on taking care of myself and give it all I had.

It all boils down to three important questions you need to ask yourself:

Am I willing to embrace the past?

Am I willing to put in the effort?

Am I willing to invest in myself?

In order to succeed, the answer to each one must be YES. A resounding yes makes all the difference between staying right where you are versus owning your worth, achieving optimum health of mind and body, and claiming your success.

Every aspect must be congruent for success. For instance, I can't say that I'm going to put in the effort and invest in myself but still be angry and bitter about the past. That is excess baggage, a heavy load that will hold you down. You must first free yourself before you can expect to climb out of the hole you are in.

Similarly, I can't say that I'm going to embrace the past and put in the effort but not be willing to invest in myself. To give myself the best chance to succeed, I needed to take care of my mind and body.

I was eating unhealthy, pre-diabetic, had high blood pressure and overly stressed and sleep-deprived. One by one I had to take care of all these issues in order to prime myself to fight.

Think of it like a car about to take a long, all-important trip. To be able to get to the destination safely, you'd have to make sure the tire pressures were checked, the engine oil cleaned, fluids and gasoline replenished. You needed to make sure the car was properly tuned up, or you'd have problems getting there, right?

YOU are the most important vehicle for your success. How badly do you want to get there? Then take good care of yourself. Consistently. No more excuses. No more crutches from the past.

Tune yourself up and go for the ride of your life.

IT'S NOT YOUR FAULT

If there's one thing I want you to take away from this chapter, it's this:

You CAN change your self-sabotaging core beliefs and make a difference in your life. Stop blaming yourself and putting yourself down.

Own your worth. Believe in yourself and be prepared to soar.

It CAN be done.

Once again, I ask you, "How determined are you to invest in yourself for your success and happiness?"

CHAPTER 8
#3 Create off-beaten paths

Most people know that to achieve a goal, they must plan their path toward it. You can't just wish for it, and then it happens. There is no luck or magic involved.

The problem is, 80% of people don't even set goals for themselves. What's interesting to know too is that of the 20% of people that do set a goal, around 70% are unsuccessful in achieving them.

That's crazy, right? So many try, but not many get there.

All your life, you've been constantly bombarded by family, friends, society, religion, and the media to follow, behave and live in certain ways. Have you ever thought about that?

What I want you to realize is that no two people are identical. Not even identical twins! Neither are situations in life.

With that being said, you need to find and follow your OWN true values and desires ... NOT what others EXPECT of you.

You'll never get to where you want to be if you are not willing to take a risk and create your own path. Do not be afraid of unchartered waters that can lead you to your goal.

THE TWO MOST PARALYZING FEARS

There are 2 most paralyzing fears that hold us back in life: rejection and failure.

We are afraid of being judged and criticized.

"What will people think of me? What if I don't succeed? What will they say?"

Fear stops us from stepping out of our comfort zone, from exploring the unknown, from daring to change. We get stuck with self-limiting beliefs and self-sabotage.

Examples of these are reluctance to try new things or accept a challenge, procrastination, not following through with what you set out to do, excessive anxiety, thinking *I'm not good enough,* and counting yourself out before you even try.

My past failures made me hesitant to try again. It was one thing to disappoint myself, but it was more embarrassing for me to disappoint my family, friends, or colleagues. I procrastinated because I was fearful of facing the challenge again. It made me anxious. I second-guessed myself. I was fearful of being rejected because I wasn't good enough.

Talk about being paralyzed by fear. I was afraid to do anything.

FAILURE: A MATTER OF PERSPECTIVE

Failure can either be a powerful incentive or the worst thing in the world. How you see failure makes all the difference. Failure is a matter of perspective.

There's one view: "It's the end of the world. I can't do it. I'm done."

Then there's the better view: "What valuable lesson did I learn? How can I improve? What good came about this?"

For example, you discover who your true friends are; you become aware of how strong a person you are; you find unexpected ideas or inspiration to succeed.

Allow failure to be your best teacher. It teaches a multitude of lessons if you keep an open mind and do not let it drag you down. Learn from them. Let that newfound insight or knowledge serve as your fuel, your powerful incentive to try again—this time, armed with more wisdom and confidence.

NO STRAIGHT PATH TO SUCCESS

There is NO straight path to success, and no cookie cutter pattern either. There are, however, proven strategies and principles that can save you years of pain and get you results even faster.

My client Vivian is a young wife, mother of 2, and now a very successful entrepreneur. Her past was ridden with previous business failures. They were hard pills to swallow, and disappointments were not easy to recover from.

Her goal was to help her husband augment their income. She came to me discouraged and afraid to try again.

By helping her discover her self-worth, true passion, new mindset toward past failures, she found the courage to try a different path toward her goal. She realized where mistakes were made, embraced them as valuable learning opportunities and carefully plotted a different approach.

She now owns and operates a successful, growing business and has plenty of time to enjoy with her family.

The only way failure can stop us is if we let it.

There is more than one path to a destination. Think of a GPS system. There are main roads and side roads. Some get you there quicker; some not as fast. The point is, by understanding your past—and with perseverance—you will get there.

Customize your road and travel through it without fear.

There is a beautiful quote that sums this up perfectly. It was said by Zero Dean, author of *Not Everyone Will Understand Your Journey*. I want to share it with you to give you courage ...

"One's unique road to success is often revealed by the lessons learned from failed attempts to navigate without a path."

Powerful and true. It's a great reminder for all of us to keep in mind.

Have the courage to find your path and go for it.

You WILL get there.

CHAPTER 9
#4 Sink or swim tenacity

How fierce is your determination to keep from drowning? To survive? To succeed? To be the best you can be? That is the sink or swim tenacity you need to have.

AMMUNITION TO SUCCEED

There are three crucial factors that determine the likelihood of success.

The first is your motivation for change. Second, your behavior toward your goal. Third, your willpower.

How driven are you to make a change? How badly do you want it? How much effort are you going to give? It follows the 'all or none' principle. Half-baked efforts will only delay success and lead to frustration.

How focused and driven are you to work toward your goal?

How tenacious will you be when the going gets tough?

What will achieving your goals mean to you physically, mentally, emotionally, and spiritually?

How much ammunition do you have now within you to make this happen?

THE CRITICAL FACTOR

The most critical step and most significant factor for change is willpower.

Studies in human psychology show that higher strength of willpower correlates to higher self-esteem, greater physical and mental health, less bing-eating and substance abuse, better relationship skills, better savings behavior and financial security.

Think about that for a moment.

EVERYONE who has ever been successful in their career, their business, their sport, in fulfilling their dream all have one common denominator. A tenacious willpower.

Let me expand on this further.

Lack of willpower is the top reason why people fall short of their goals to make lifestyle changes such as losing weight, exercising regularly, saving money, quitting unhealthy habits, and following through with their plans.

It's like a New Year's resolution that is repeated each year because it never got done. Been there, done that ... right?

It sets you up to feel hopeless about improving your life and also feel incapable of achieving much and/or unworthy of your goal.

The good news is that willpower can strengthen over time and is a renewable resource.

The million-dollar question is, "How can I strengthen and renew my willpower?"

The answer may surprise you, and this is where the beauty of science comes in.

Willpower can be strengthened and replenished by simply taking care of your body.

The reason why understanding your body and taking care of yourself is so important in mastering this sink or swim mentality is because once you do, you'll be able to identify situations or people that drain your willpower and know how to deal with them.

Those are the people you should be pulling away from instead of spending most of your time with, if at all. If they drain you of energy and drive, this cannot be a helpful situation.

You can learn how to build up your mental power to overcome stressful and difficult challenges that come your way. Nothing can stop you when your mind is strong, focused and unshakable.

You can learn how to replenish and boost your willpower when it has been exhausted without beating yourself down.

Willpower is very much like muscles. It's actually a simple concept. When we strengthen our muscles; we perform better physically. The same goes for willpower.

Let me tell you something about your amazing brain:

The center for your willpower, decision-making, self-control and behavior regulation is in the area of your brain called the prefrontal cortex. That's right behind your forehead.

When you strengthen this area by eating healthy and getting enough sleep, it allows it to recharge—helping you make sound decisions, have better control against unhealthy urges and recharges your willpower.

Willpower Gets Stronger When Exercised

We can do that by exercising some level of self-control every day. Set reasonable, simple goals and get them done.

Let me share mine with you: I set a 10 p.m. bedtime every night, 5:30 a.m. wake up each morning, spend 10 minutes in prayer or meditation after waking up and make sure I eat breakfast. Every day. Simple and doable.

Exercising your willpower makes it easier for you to accomplish other tasks you set out to do.

Willpower Is Fueled By Glucose In Your Body

It is very important to know that both physical AND mental activity in the human body depends on and uses energy in the form of glucose. It is the fuel for our body and brain.

When we have low levels of glucose, it weakens our self-control, focus, and brain power. Low levels of glucose also increase impulsivity—not thinking things through—causing erratic decisions that may take us farther away from achieving our success.

Self-control, focus, and brain power can be overworked, making it weak or depleted of energy until it recovers.

Allow me to teach you a little more about your amazing human body.

Each cell of your body is equipped with a powerhouse called the mitochondria. It generates most of the energy our body needs by converting what we eat into fuel for our cells called ATP, adenosine triphosphate. This big word, simply put, stands for body fuel.

The human body constantly needs ATP to function properly, and that includes the brain. Because of that, any dysfunction of the mitochondria can negatively affect our mental function, which includes self-control or willpower.

In order to recover, you need to get it back to the best state possible so it can recharge. How? By making sure you get the proper nutrition, the right amount of sleep and take control over stress.

Speaking of stress, it the biggest energy drainer of all for both your mind and body. It affects sleep, your eating habits and triggers cellular changes in your brain which actually makes it harder to accomplish any task as well as weakens your will.

By training your willpower, strengthening your mind with proper food and sleep without medications, and allowing yourself to recharge and de-stress, you can become focused and unwavering in your will to succeed.

I used to be sleep-deprived, sedentary; I wasn't making healthy food choices and constantly lived in stress. I was a walking recipe for disaster: pre-diabetic, had high blood pressure, depressed, constantly worrying and not getting much sleep.

It was no wonder that I struggled to get things done. I was wiped out physically, mentally, emotionally.

The moment I recognized what needed to be done and took care of myself consistently, the changes were incredible. I am busier than ever now but manage to stay driven, focused and productive with significantly less stress. I have a whole lot more energy and am happier than I've ever been.

UNLEASHING THE POWER WITHIN

Mahatma Gandhi's words resonate with me loud and clear. "Strength does not come from physical capacity. It comes from indomitable will."

The only thing that stands between you and what you want in your life is your will to change and move forward in that direction.

The power is in your hands.

Remember: sink or swim tenacity, like your survival depended on it.

How much you accomplish and how soon you succeed rests on an unrelenting will and focused drive.

It took me years to learn my lessons and get to this point, but better late than never. I look back then, see myself now and tell myself, "What a ride this has been!"

Time is valuable and irreplaceable. You can never get it back.

Unleash your power within and seize every day like it was your last. You'll be amazed by how far you'll go.

CHAPTER 10

#5 Invest in a mentor

You may be wondering, *What's so good about investing in a mentor?*

If you are a Star Wars fan, think of your mentor as Yoda.

A mentor empowers you to visualize a possible future and believe it can be achieved. You can do anything you truly set your mind to.

I have worked with amazing mentors, each with their own gifts to share.

My first mentor opened my mind to something I didn't have the courage to do. The more I visualized that future, the more I believed I could do it. In 3 months, I wrote my very first book, *Turn Diabetes Around,* which became a #1 bestseller in less than a year. Through that book, I have helped countless families with diabetes and have now reached people around the world.

If someone told me I'd be able to do that in the past, I would have thought that to be one of the biggest jokes ever.

What made the difference? She helped me believe that I could do it.

Since then, I have invested in other mentors, depending on my needs and their own unique strengths. My current mentor shared with me powerful insights that gave me the courage to step beyond my level of comfort, write this book, reach out to even more people and spread my wings further. The growth and progress I have experienced with him is priceless.

I want you to know this fact: the best and most successful people in the world ALL have a mentor.

A mentor is your greatest ally for success.

BENEFITS

Mentoring is a brain to pick, an ear to listen, and a push in the right direction. A good mentor will ALWAYS have your best interest in mind as you work together to get to your goal.

Working with a mentor creates a sense of partnership so you do not feel alone or isolated. This is reassuring in so many ways because, let's face it, it's a great feeling to know that there is someone who will surely be by your side to guide you; someone who can encourage you when you're overwhelmed; someone who can think clearly for you when you're confused; someone who will WANT you to succeed and get you going on the right path.

A mentor is a sounding board, allowing you to be heard in a safe and confidential environment. You don't have to worry. Whatever you discuss together is just between the two of you, and you don't have to worry about being judged or criticized for speaking up. A mentor's role is to build you up and not push you down.

Another benefit is, a good mentor stretches your thinking, providing new and helpful perspectives. You benefit from their insight and vision, which comes from their wider experience over many years helping so many people. Their wisdom is also based on their own past experiences: both successes and failures.

Think of it as a safe path paved just for you.

A great mentor keeps you focused, determined and in the optimal mindset possible to get you to your goal. Your mentor becomes your compass guiding you in the right direction, saving you the time you would have lost if you didn't know the way.

People I've mentored have told me, "You are my brain on its best day." A good mentor clears the dust of self-doubt and insecurities from your mind, helping you to be the best possible version of yourself.

Knowing all this now, isn't a mentor the kind of person you'd want on your team?

DRAWBACKS

In the balance of life, there are drawbacks as much as there are benefits.

Mentorship is an expense but, if you choose wisely, will become the greatest investment you could ever give to yourself. The best mentor will get you farther than you ever thought possible.

They are not quick-fix solutions that magically change your life in a matter of days. It takes time and is an active process. You need to keep moving. You have to work and do your part.

A word of caution too: be careful who you choose. Not all mentors are the same. Not all will deliver what they promise, leaving you disappointed, disheartened, and with less money in your pocket.

You need to choose carefully and wisely. It is an investment, but a good mentor will always fight for your dreams.

I learned from the best and paid premium pricing for their services. Was it worth every penny?

Absolutely! It was the best investment I made for myself because the person I am now is light years away from the person I was: in health, wisdom, strength, and lasting happiness—both personally and professionally.

Once again, the questions I want you to really think about are:

"Do I want the best?" and "How much am I willing to invest for myself?"

VALUABLE PARTNERSHIP

Investing in a good mentor and your drive to succeed results in a force to reckon with.

They will be the best co-pilot you will have on your journey to success: redirecting your path and pointing you in the right direction.

CHAPTER 11
Priming for success

R emember that analogy to a car needing to be tuned up prior to a long, all-important journey?

You are that vehicle on your journey to success.

Every aspect of you should be prepared to perform and function optimally to get you to your destination more effectively and efficiently.

Think of each facet as individual wheels of the car: physical, mental, emotional, and spiritual. If one is flat, you won't go far. If the pressure is either too low or too high, the time to destination becomes slower or dangerous. Each wheel must be balanced and in the best form.

If one facet of your life is in crisis, all the rest are affected. Balance is crucial in priming yourself for success.

PHYSICAL

What are health problems holding you back? What are you doing to eliminate or significantly minimize the effects of your condition on your body? How diligent and consistent are you in taking care of your health issues?

Are you eating right? Getting enough sleep? Do you smoke, drink alcohol, use illicit drugs? Are you constantly stressed or anxious? Are you seeing a doctor? Do you follow your doctor's advice?

No matter how strong you are mentally, if your physical body is struggling with health issues, performance and endurance eventually become a concern.

My health was in jeopardy, and my family medical history put me at high risk, so I was determined to take action. I cleaned my diet, exercised regularly and learned to eliminate or better handle whatever caused me tremendous stress. In the process, I lost weight, was no longer pre-diabetic, came off medications for high blood pressure, and relocated to start a new job where I am happy and at peace.

I have more energy now than ever before and have eliminated many health problems that dragged me down in the past.

MENTAL

Your frame of mind is a powerful force behind your ability to achieve what you want. Are you focused? Are you well rested each day? Is your mind calm and engaged or chaotic and confused? Do you struggle to stay on track?

What are setbacks that impede your performance? Are you sleep-deprived? Are you easily distracted? Are you multitasking and overwhelmed?

A clouded, overwhelmed and exhausted mind is a recipe for disappointment and frustration. A clear and focused mind gets the job done quickly and effectively.

Practicing the principles I teach my clients has made a tremendous difference in my life as well as theirs.

Notice that I use the word practice. This is not a onetime deal that once you get it, you'll never lose it. Mental tenacity takes deliberate, disciplined practice every single day to keep it sharp and functioning like a well-oiled machine.

My habits to take care of my mind and brain include ensuring at least 7 hours of sleep at night, abstinence from alcohol, learning something new or working on worthwhile projects as well as allowing myself downtime when signs of fatigue set in. I resort to aromatherapy, listen to classical music, meditate, have a candlelit bath, play the piano, sing, or take a walk with my dog.

As you can see, it's nothing extravagant. Consistent practice every day can significantly cut down your recovery time when stress sets in.

EMOTIONAL

How do you handle stress, delays, disappointments, frustration?

Are you easily discouraged? Do you become critical of yourself? Are you quick to blame yourself or others? Do you easily lose hope? Do you have a tendency toward feeling depressed?

What about success and praise?

Does it make you more assertive and inspired? Or do you tend to get ccomfortable and complacent? Does it drive you to keep on going relentlessly? Or does it tend to make you slow down and rest on your laurels for extended periods?

How you handle the roadblocks and triumphs determines how quickly you can get to your goals.

I have long learned to stop being critical of myself. I make a mistake; I learn. It's not the end of the world.

Remember the segment on pain? It is not a personal vendetta against you. It is your biggest teacher with so many opportunities to learn. When my clients get this, their insight transforms from doom and gloom to hopeful courage. They become warriors who learn to stand strong.

As for success and praise, let it be your fuel. Keep moving forward. Don't ever stagnate. Life is too short. Embrace every moment to grow and improve.

SPIRITUAL

Many successful people acknowledge a higher force where they derive strength and inspiration, and who they give gratitude to. A strong faith also is instrumental in helping many survive even the most painful or difficult trials.

Whether it's a religion or personal spiritual belief, it is always helpful to have a powerful source of strength in your life's journey.

I relied on my faith when I hit rock bottom in 2008. It was my lifeline when it felt like I had nothing else to hold on to, to keep from drowning.

Find strength in whatever you believe in, or whatever inspires you. It can surely move mountains.

THE POWER OF GRATITUDE

Trust me on this: In gratitude, you will find strength.

Gratitude is my lifeline. In my most difficult moments, it is the powerful ammunition I rely on to boost my spirits and fuel my will to succeed.

It puts everything in perspective, and suddenly, your burdens seem easier to bear.

When I give thanks, I recognize the blessings I take for granted and realize that I don't have it so bad after all. It is a humbling experience.

It may be as simple as "Thank you for another new day, my loving children, a roof over my head, food on the table, my steady job, my health."

You are abundantly blessed. All you have to do is open your eyes, lift up your heart and feel it—no matter how small. Every single day.

CHAPTER 12
Your move, your choice

The five shifts you've just learned are ammunition you need to stop apathy in its tracks and take control over it.

It all begins with owning your worth with no apologies, speaking your truth with no fear, planning your own unique path where no one else has traveled, and fighting for your dream with unwavering tenacity.

Remember, you don't have to go through this alone. Working with a mentor can be the very best investment you can do for yourself.

As with every great challenge, the hardest part is taking that very first step toward committing to yourself. Once you get going, momentum keeps you moving forward. The harder you work, the faster you'll go.

My clients remind me of babies learning how to walk. In the beginning, they hesitate and are afraid to let go because they're afraid to fall.

Falling is inevitable, but with practice comes skill. Next thing you know, they only hold on to you by one finger. Then they let go. Once they realize what they've done and succeeded, they become practically unstoppable.

Nothing brings me greater joy than to see my clients transform before my eyes and soar. That's when I realize I've done my job and taught them well.

Your opportunity awaits.

The choice is yours. What will it be?

Let's put an end to apathy and be the best we can be for ourselves, our loved ones, our community, and our world.

If you're curious to learn more, please visit my website at <u>margamaciasmd.com</u> for information on current and upcoming programs, events, and webinars. There you will also have the opportunity to sign up for a free consultation with me if you are thinking about working with me one-on-one to maximize your results or as a group. After you apply, if we are a good fit, get ready to fasten your seatbelt. I will take you under my wing and get you on track to claim your birthright and start living the life of your dreams.

I also invite you to join my private Facebook group of fellow Birthright Conquerors. You can meet others who are using this method and can share their experiences and triumphs with you. Join us at www.facebook.com/groups/ClaimYourBirthright.

You may also email me at marga@margamaciasmd.com for questions or to share your success story with me. I would love to hear from you!

ABOUT THE AUTHOR

DR. **MARGA MACIAS** is a #1 best-selling author, speaker and expert advisor to doctors, CEOs, business owners, moms and dads with indomitable spirits. Dr. Macias was born in the Philippines, in a little province up in the mountains of Baguio City. She was the firstborn to young doctors of very humble beginnings, both going after their dreams overseas. For the first seven years of her life, she grew up in the United States until her family moved back to the Philippines.

She followed in their footsteps and earned her medical degree in the Philippines in 1989 at the age of twenty-four. Pediatrics was the specialty of choice she pursued because of her love for children, and she continued on to complete a subspecialty training in Pediatric Critical Care in Illinois, USA.

Dr. Marga Macias has helped 150,000 patients and counting and has saved the lives of more than five thousand children and adults while working in hospitals, intensive care units, and clinics.

As a blessed mother of 2 children, she had to end her marriage of seven years due to physical abuse. She became a single mom at the height of her highly stressful subspecialty training and found herself alone and struggling to make ends meet.

In January 2008, after suffering depression, being undervalued and underpaid, Dr. Macias faced a crucial turning point. She was flown to the University of Maryland Neurosurgical Intensive Care Unit for emergency brain surgery. An undetected aneurysm had ruptured.

Four weeks later, she lost her beloved father to cancer, and she hit what she called 'rock bottom.'

Surviving the aneurysm was a wakeup call. Given a second chance, she dedicated herself to one mission: making an impact in this world and leaving a legacy for her children.

She relocated her family to New Mexico where she has found peace and meaning as a pediatrician. Her children have since grown and are thriving in their chosen careers.

Her #1 best-selling book, *Turn Diabetes Around,* continues to change lives around the world as she helps fight diabetes. Dr. Macias' Turn Diabetes Around Facebook page has followers worldwide who are inspired by her teachings and mentorship toward this cause.

Her new book *Birthright: 5 Secrets to Reclaim the Power of You* is aimed to conquer a new enemy: Apathy. It is her desire to help millions of readers harness the greatness they were born with, to live the life of their dreams.

She currently resides in Roswell, New Mexico where she is a beloved pediatrician with a very successful practice at BCA Medical Associates. Her strength and resilience have inspired her children who are now successful individuals, poised to make their own difference in this world.

ACKNOWLEDGEMENT

To my dearest darlings, my children, Paolo and Mika, thank you for being my rock. You have been my source of strength through my most painful trials as well as my constant stream of love and inspiration. I am grateful beyond measure to have you in my life and love you forever.

To my parents, Peny and Chona, thank you for teaching me dedication, perseverance, and integrity. I remember your struggles as I was growing up, but you continued on and gave my siblings and me a life many could only dream of. Dad, thank you for teaching me true compassion. There is no greater honor than for someone to say I'm just like you in that way. Mom, thank you for teaching me how to never give up. I am proud to have found my own strength by your example. I love you both with all my heart.

To my mentors, thank you for believing in me. You helped me see the gift within me that only needed to be unearthed and polished. Thank you for sharing your gems of wisdom and for preparing me to soar as far and high as I dare to fly.

To my steadfast and loyal best friends ... you know who you are. Thank you for helping me stand when the weight of my trials seemed too hard to bear. Your presence, love, and support helped keep me from sinking, and the laughter and joy you bring on better days are nourishment for my heart and spirit.

Finally, to You, my Almighty God, I give honor and praise. You never left my side. Even in my deepest, darkest hours, You were always there walking beside me or lifting me when I thought I could go no further. In Your infinite wisdom, I now realize how every obstacle You put in my path are stepping stones toward a clearer, brighter, happier future when I put my trust in You. How truly wonderful are Your ways. Thank You so much for the bountiful blessings in my life.

Made in the USA
Coppell, TX
06 November 2022

85893725R00081